REAL WORLD EC

How a
Recession
Works

Jeanne Nagle

+6.73

+1.33

+21.64
+1483   +9.19
+324
+32.47   +11.02
+235
+41   +35.05
+021
+242
+556

ROSEN
PUBLISHING

New York

*To my parents, Barb and Jim, who have shared
their wise money management skills*

Published in 2010 by The Rosen Publishing Group, Inc.
29 East 21st Street, New York, NY 10010

First Edition

Library of Congress Cataloging-in-Publication Data

Nagle, Jeanne M.
How a recession works / Jeanne Nagle.
    p. cm.—(Real world economics)
Includes bibliographical references and index.
ISBN-13: 978-1-4358-5321-8 (library binding)
1. Recessions—United States. 2. Business cycles—United States.
3. Economic indicators—United States. 4. United States—Economic
policy. I. Title.
HB3743.N338 2010
338.5'42—dc22

2008049264

Manufactured in the United States of America

CPSIA Compliance Information: Batch #BR902021YA: For futher information contact Windmill Books, New York, New York at
1-866-478-0556.

On the cover: A store in New York City advertises a post-Christmas going-
out-of-business sale. As the economy slid into a recession in 2008, consumers
stopped spending money, and many businesses suffered and failed.

Contents

INTRODUCTION | | | |

The first years of the twenty-first century were a time of overall prosperity in the United States. A large portion of the country's population had plenty of money or were able to borrow easily from banks and other lending companies. They were not hesitant to spend what they had either. Using loans from banks and credit cards, people purchased many goods and services, especially expensive new houses.

After several years of this positive, thriving economy, however, Americans started to sense a change in the economic atmosphere. Beginning in late 2006, signs of an economic slowdown in the United States started popping up. A slowdown is when the rate of economic activity decreases. It seems that Americans had spent money faster than they could earn it. Now that the time had come to return loans and pay off credit cards, many people found themselves deeply in debt. This made it hard for them to buy anything else, so their spending decreased. Other consumers noticed this, too, and became nervous that the same thing might happen to them. Therefore, they also cut way back on their spending.

This slowdown generated many discussions in the media and debate among economists, who study the buying and selling of goods and services, about whether or not the country had entered a recession. This is when the economy experiences negative growth in total output for at least two consecutive quarters, or six months. Economists and politicians had a hard time deciding what this slowdown meant. Yet many average U.S. citizens, who felt the effects of decreased economic activity, were certain that the country had officially entered a period of recession.

Just the idea that a recession might be looming on the horizon is enough to put people on edge. That's because there are several negative effects associated with a slowdown in economic growth. During a recession, companies sell fewer goods and services. As a result, companies lay off workers because they no longer need them. Having fewer workers also lowers a

Trouble paying bills is just one of the issues that arises during a lengthy economic downturn, or recession.

company's costs. Still, some companies go out of business. When people lose their jobs, the unemployment rate rises.

A recession is a decrease in economic activity that causes a rise in the unemployment rate. When people are not working,

they are less likely to spend money on goods and services, especially luxury items. This hurts the businesses that make these goods and services. But recessions may not necessarily be a cause for concern. In fact, they are a normal part of what's known as the business cycle. The economy naturally experiences ups and downs. A recession is an example of a down period. Given time, money matters may correct themselves and start swinging back up after a slowdown.

Problems arise when the economy stays down for too long and too many people are negatively affected. When this happens, the government and businesses often give money back to citizens in the form of tax cuts, reduced interest rates on loans, or store sales. These measures are meant to help people start spending again and boost the economy back into the more healthy part of the business-cycle rhythm.

Knowing why they happen, and understanding what's likely to happen when an economic slowdown hits, can make experiencing a recession a lot less scary and getting through it a lot easier.

7

CHAPTER ONE

What a Recession Is and Isn't

To understand what it means to be in a recession, it helps to understand some basic economic concepts. Economies throughout the world revolve around the idea of "value." Something is considered valuable if it is precious or special. People want or need things that are considered valuable. In economic terms, an item's value can relate to the supply and demand for the object.

When merchandise is rare or even one of a kind, like a famous artist's painting, it is considered valuable partly because there is a limited supply of this item. If an athlete is better, stronger, or faster than other players, he or she is especially valuable to the team. This will result in a great demand for the athlete and often a high salary.

What Does Value Have to Do with a Recession?

Simply put, a recession is when the value of what a country has to offer—to its own citizens and those of other nations—

Museums display and guard rare artwork because it is considered valuable. Value is a controlling factor during a period of recession.

decreases for at least several months. This is when a nation's economy recedes, or pulls back, from its normal buying and selling patterns. In other words, people hold back from spending as much money as they normally would or demand fewer goods and services. As a result, businesses scale back on the products they make available for sale, also known as their supply of goods and services.

Buying and selling patterns are determined primarily by examining a country's gross domestic product (GDP). This economic indicator can be calculated by adding up all the money spent on goods and services in a country. It includes products bought by households, business investments, government purchases, and net exports (goods and services sold to other countries minus the goods and services bought from other countries). All goods and services created and offered on American soil (any of the fifty states, the District of Columbia, and the five U.S. territories) are included in the United States' GDP.

Items made in America, or by American companies operating in foreign countries, are part of the United States' gross national product. Imported items or products made in the United States by foreign companies, like these Toyota cars, are not part of the GNP.

Another economic statistic that refers to total output is the gross national product (or GNP). The GNP measures the total amount of goods and services produced by Americans. So, this number would include cars manufactured in Detroit, Michigan, and cars produced in foreign countries by American companies.

Each nation assigns a government agency to keep track of the figures that make up the GDP. In the United States, this task is the responsibility of the Bureau of Economic Analysis. During a recession, the numbers collected by the bureau show that the GDP is declining, or on a downward curve. This is also referred to as negative growth. When studying GDP trends, economists look at "real GDP." Nominal GDP is the number that is calculated by adding up all money spent on goods and services. Real GDP is the nominal GDP adjusted to take into account changes in the price level. By adjusting the GDP, economists can compare GDP levels from one quarter to the next, without worrying that changing price levels are misrepresenting the data.

Notice that the economy needs to move downward for at least six to nine months for there to be a recession. Sometimes, the GDP numbers are low but remain flat at about the same level for months, showing no sign of moving down or up. This is a different economic phenomenon known as stagnation. Likewise, if a country experiences negative growth for only a quarter and then has positive growth the next two quarters, the economy is not considered to have been in a recession.

The Domino Effect

Though they often disagree on exactly when a recession has started, economists do agree on how a recession acts once it has begun. First, and most important, the rate at which people spend money slows down. This slowdown may begin in only one business sector, or field of work, at first. Eventually, the lag in spending spreads to other sectors because the economy is interdependent. That means different types of businesses are connected, so what affects one business affects many others as well.

This is called the domino effect. If you line up domino tiles and tip the first one over, it knocks over the next, which knocks over the next, and so on. Sectors of the economy react in much the same way during a recession. When one type of business topples, it usually shakes, and possibly completely knocks over, others.

For instance, if cars aren't selling well, then the manufacturer will not make as many vehicles. Car companies will then lay off workers because there isn't enough for them to do and because costs need to be lowered. The unemployed auto workers no longer have enough money coming in to buy things, such as new clothes. If enough people stop buying new clothes, the clothing industry experiences a slowdown in sales. This could result in laying off more workers. A small clothing store may even lose enough sales that it is forced to go out of business, which means more people are out of a job. The more unemployed workers there are, the fewer people there are to strengthen the economy through consumer spending. This, in turn, leads to more pressure on stores and manufacturers, and more layoffs. It's a vicious cycle.

Global Recessions

The domino effect can be a very real factor in the world economy. While each nation has its own financial system that is managed independently, those systems also are interdependent. This means that they rely on each other for their well-being and smooth functioning, through a process known as economic globalization. This involves connections made between businesses and marketplaces around the world. Trade (imports and exports), foreign investments, and international banking are tools of economic globalization.

Just as economic slowdowns can spread from one business sector to another, a recession that starts in one country can affect the economies of financially interdependent nations. This can eventually cause a global recession. For instance, less spending in the United States doesn't lower only America's GDP. It also slows the economies of countries that export products to the United States. This is because they depend on sales to the United States to boost their own economic activity.

The closing of one factory can have a ripple effect around the world. Lost jobs in one country mean fewer customers for companies everywhere.

During a global recession, there will be a decline in the gross world product (GWP). This is the amount of all goods and services produced around the world added together. But exactly how fast and far the decline in the GWP should be in order

to declare a global recession hasn't been established. The International Monetary Fund (IMF), a financial monitoring organization, estimates that the global economy (as measured by the GWP) would grow by only 3 percent or less during a worldwide recession. According to the IMF's measurement, the last global recession occurred in 2001–2002.

The Business Cycle

What many people don't realize is that recessions are a normal part of the way the economy works. The movement of the economy is called the business cycle.

If you were to make a chart showing economic activity over the course of a year, it would look like a wavy line or a small mountain range, complete with hills and valleys. That's because the business cycle goes through a series of ups, called peaks, and downs, known as troughs. When the cycle is on its way up, the economy is experiencing more growth than usual. It is said to be going through an expansion. The economy is said to go through a contraction when it is on its way down.

The contractions that happen during the normal business cycle are actually recessions.

In a way, contractions are how the economy cools itself down after it has heated up and expanded too much. Expansions,

Breadlines, where people waited for a free meal of soup and bread, were common during the Great Depression, which started in 1929.

likewise, are how the economy recovers and climbs back up after experiencing a trough. The economy works best when it has this fluid, moderate up-and-down motion. It is as if constantly changing creates a kind of balance and stability.

Over the course of a normal business cycle, the contractions, or recessions, usually are not too severe, and they correct themselves fairly quickly. According to the National Bureau of Economic Research (NBER), recessions generally last, on average, about a year.

Recession vs. Depression

Within the business cycle, a depression is more than a contraction. It is most definitely a trough. A depression is a major economic decline, where people struggle to pay for the basic necessities of life, such as food and shelter.

Economists use the GDP to help gauge whether a slowdown is a recession or a depression. A decline of less than 10 percent in the GDP is considered a recession. In the 1970s, the United States

17

economy experienced a slowdown that economists now agree was a true recession. Over two years, from 1973 to 1975, the country's GDP fell nearly 5 percent. A 10 percent decrease in the GDP signals a depression. During the well-known Great Depression—one of the darkest times in United States economic history that lasted throughout the 1930s—the GDP dropped about 30 percent at its lowest point. Even as the economy was working its way out of trouble, the decline in the GDP stayed above the 10 percent threshold.

Recessions and depressions are related in that they are both part of the downward curve of the business cycle. The difference is that recessions aren't as deep or long-lived as depressions. Also, while recessions always come before depressions, because the economy can't jump right from a peak to a deep trough, not all recessions turn into depressions.

MYTHS and FACTS

MYTH   The business cycle is a fairly regular series of economic ups and downs.

FACT   The business cycle does show peaks and troughs in the economy, but it is by no means regular or consistent. Recessions can be lengthy or short, as can the time between them. That's why recessions are so hard to predict.

MYTH   The stock market is the most important indicator in determining whether or not the country is in a recession.

FACT   Watching the stock market is helpful in that it reflects economic health and consumer confidence, but it is not the most important indicator. A nation's GDP and employment rate give a much better overall picture of an economic slowdown.

MYTH   Recessions are disastrous for the economy.

FACT   How negatively a recession affects the economy depends on how long and deep it is. Over the past twenty years, recessions have been relatively short and mild. In between those troughs, the United States experienced great growth. Recessions can be merely the economy balancing itself after extreme growth, rather than signaling a crisis or disaster.

19

CHAPTER TWO

The Causes of a Recession

The world of economics is ruled by the law of supply and demand. The law of supply and demand is a "law" based upon typical economic activity that maps out how buyers and sellers act on their own and react to each other.

Supply and demand also have a direct effect on the business cycle. The relationship between the availability of products and people wanting to purchase those goods and services is responsible for the business cycle's expansions and contractions. That connection, along with both unwelcome interruptions, known as "shocks," and the way a nation's government handles its money supply, can ultimately determine whether or not a country experiences a recession.

Changes in the Marketplace

The law of supply and demand states that the value of a good or service changes according to how much of that given product is available (the supply) as well as how much people want it (demand). Supply and demand influence the price people pay for goods and services in the marketplace.

For instance, if the supply of a product, or the amount available, is high, then the product is not rare. Remember, value is connected to how rare or precious something is. Consequently, the item's price will be low when its supply, or availability, is high. Likewise, the price of an item increases when it is in short supply.

Also, the more popular or useful an item is, the more people will demand it. Initially, the high demand will result in a short

People will camp out to get limited supplies of popular new items, like Apple's iPhone. Demand skyrockets, and production increases.

supply of the product. Think about the long lines of hopeful customers that formed outside of electronics and computer stores when the latest versions of PlayStation, Nintendo Wii, or the iPhone were released. Many people went home empty-handed. When that happens, a business eventually increases production to meet the growing demand.

Increased production comes at a cost, though. Companies need to hire more workers and use more materials as they boost their supplies by making more products. To get back some of the money they're spending on additional employee wages and extra materials, businesses often mark up the price of their merchandise. This helps them make a profit. Money earned from the sale of a product beyond what it costs to create and sell that product is called profit. As long as production costs go up, prices typically will go up as well.

Depending on how strong the demand for goods and services is, and how much money customers can earn or borrow to pay for their purchases, everything may run smoothly in this way for months or even years. Yet, true to the law of supply and demand, higher prices eventually result in decreased demand for a good or service because many people will be either unable or unwilling to pay the higher price.

In 2007, gas prices started to soar. By July 17, gas was selling at its highest level ever—$4.11 per gallon. People responded by lowering their demand for gas. Rather than drive their own cars, people took public transportation, walked, or joined a carpool. By October, demand had decreased by 10 percent compared to the previous year. Less demand caused gas prices to drop, and on October 7, 2008, gas was selling for $3.48 per gallon.

A "Sticky" Situation

When demand for goods and services goes down, the marketplace tries to restore balance by slowing down or contracting. Prices drop, and items go on sale in the hope of selling off the supply that has built up when demand was high. Production slows down. However, there are some areas of the economy that resist quick correction. Some costs of doing business remain high even as the rest of the economy contracts. These areas are said to be "sticky" because during periods of economic contraction, they get stuck at expansion levels.

Wages and income are examples of this "stickiness." Workers are hired at salary levels that reflect the current economy. If an expansion is under way, then starting wages will be higher than normal. When a slowdown occurs, businesses might offer lower salaries to new employees, but wages for those who are already employed do not automatically go down. People keep earning the salary that was agreed upon when they were first hired. Companies are more likely to lay off workers than try to reduce sticky wages.

Another example of economic stickiness concerns so-called menu costs. The best example of this type of stickiness is the price list on restaurant menus. Once prices are set and put into a printed, semipermanent form, such as on menus or in brochures, businesses cannot easily change them to reflect an economic contraction. The cost of redoing printed materials every time the economy changes would cause more damage to a business than simply leaving prices high.

Sticky wages and prices that cannot drop as fast as the economy contracts put a serious glitch in the business cycle.

They can result in not hiring workers or laying off workers, which can worsen the economic contraction.

Shocks to the System

Sometimes, the economy can be performing well and expanding when suddenly a major event comes along that throws the business cycle off course, pushing a country toward recession. These events, called economic shocks, include natural disasters, such as hurricanes and earthquakes; armed conflicts and wars; the introduction of expensive government programs; and difficulty obtaining nonrenewable natural resources, such as oil.

When shocks occur, money that normally would build up a nation's economy is instead spent taking care of issues surrounding the event. For example, in 2005, Hurricane Katrina devastated New Orleans and much of the Gulf Coast, resulting in 1,836 deaths and an estimated $81.2 billion in damage. The U.S. government had to aid in the cleanup and recovery using funds that it raised through taxes and donations from average citizens. Disaster and humanitarian relief is necessary spending, yet it comes at a steep cost. When money is used for economic shocks, it is not used for something else. It's as if you were saving for an iPod but then your car broke down, so you had to sink all of your savings into auto repairs instead.

Inflation

It might be hard to understand how having more money in circulation could cause a slowdown in the economy, but it's true. The law of supply and demand affects cold, hard cash as

Natural disasters like Hurricane Katrina shock people with their devastation. They also disrupt national and individual spending plans, shocking the economy.

much as any other good or service. So, the more money that is in circulation—meaning spread out among the public—the less valuable each bill and coin becomes because of the high supply. When money becomes less valuable, it takes more of it

Having stacks of money is generally a good thing. But when a government prints too many bills, the bills lose value and inflation sets in.

to buy stuff. This is inflation—a time when there's plenty of money to go around, but it doesn't buy as much as it once did.

Inflation means that prices rise to make up for the value of money going down. An item may be worth one dollar, but a

dollar bill has dropped in value and is now worth only fifty cents. Therefore, it takes two dollar bills (each worth one dollar before inflation) to buy the item now. This 50 percent inflation rate has raised the price of a one-dollar product to two dollars, while each of those dollars can buy only half of what they used to. Each dollar has lost half of its former purchasing power.

Governments are primarily responsible for bringing about inflation, which makes trouble for their own economies. Just like individual citizens, countries must have cash to pay for the things they need, including roads and bridges, education, research, and programs such as Medicare and homeland security. Unlike ordinary people, however, the federal government has a great deal of control over its money supply. When a

War—What Is It Good For?

Throughout history, wars have been known to stimulate, or speed up, the economy instead of slowing it down. In fact, many historians believe that military spending during World War II helped the United States rebound from that ultimate

Military plane production during World War II was partly responsible for pulling the U.S. economy out of a severe depression.

economic slowdown, the Great Depression.

Oddly enough, wars can be good for the economy, at least in their early stages. Feeding, clothing, and otherwise taking care of the troops pumps money into a nation's GDP. Manufacturing and purchasing weapons creates jobs in the industrial and defense sectors. Over time, however, conflicts can be a drain on the economy. The money being spent on defense costs gets siphoned away from other areas of the economy and business sectors. Sometimes, governments even have to borrow money from other countries in order to be able to continue to pay their war expenses. This increases their national debt and puts a further break on other kinds of spending that could stimulate the economy and head off a recession.

nation runs short on money, the government can simply print and stamp more. The government inflates, or increases, the money supply to meet its needs. This trick doesn't last long, though, because eventually the law of supply and demand catches up with the government, in the form of inflation. The more money that gets printed, the less each bill is worth.

The Effect of Rising Prices

Inflation's effect on a recession has a lot to do with the behavior of consumers in response to rising prices. Some people will slow down their spending pretty quickly because items are

Luxury items like the jewelry seen here are the first to see reduced sales when inflation hits.

too expensive. Others will keep buying products no matter what the cost because there is a large supply of money still available to them—either through wages that have risen to reflect the higher cost of living or through banks with plenty of cash to lend.

Eventually, however, inflation causes people to pull back on spending, mostly because their wages can't keep up with rising prices. Less spending creates a contraction in the business cycle, and the economy cools off and slows down.

CHAPTER THREE

Predicting and Identifying a Recession

The first step in determining whether or not the economy is in a recession is to listen to what the economic experts have to say. Even if they don't agree on all the details, they are generally in synch when it comes to the big picture and the main ideas behind recessions. There are also private groups and governmental agencies all over the world whose job is to determine what's going on with the economy.

You can also watch for signs of a slowdown yourself. There are a number of economic indicators, or markers, that can act as red flags, warning you that a recession is coming or has already arrived. By listening and watching, you'll have a better idea of the economic situation in the world at large and in your own life.

The U.S. Federal Reserve

When it comes to national money matters, the Federal Reserve is the recognized authority within the United States.

The Treasury Building, in Washington, D.C., is as impressive and powerful as the Treasury Department's role in the U.S. government. The U.S. Treasury prints and circulates the nation's money.

The Federal Reserve, often referred to simply as the Fed, is the country's central bank. The federal government and all other financial institutions in America use the Fed as their bank, just like you use the local branch of your bank. The

central bank gets most of its money from interest earned on government securities, including U.S. savings bonds and treasury bills. In 2005, this amount totaled $28.96 billion. The Federal Reserve also receives money from interest earned on foreign investments and on loans to banks, as well as services provided to other banks, such as check clearing. The Fed turns all its money over to the U.S. Treasury for safekeeping, minus its operating expenses.

An independent organization that operates within the United States government but is not considered a government agency, the Fed is watched over by the U.S. Congress and run by a board that is appointed by the president. As part of its job, the board analyzes the economy and makes policy recommendations. As head of the board, the Fed chairman delivers a report on the state of the economy to Congress twice a year.

The Fed's job is to oversee the country's banking operations and make sure that the economy stays healthy. It does this by trying to ensure that overall demand equals potential supply within the economy. Therefore, it does not so much determine whether a recession has begun as try to keep normal business-cycle contractions as short as possible.

To accomplish this, the Fed uses interest rates. During periods of rising inflation, the Fed can raise interest rates to keep the economy in check. And during economic contractions, such as a recession, the Fed lowers interest rates. Lower rates essentially mean it costs less to borrow money. With low interest rates, the fee for borrowing money is less. The hope is that consumers will feel more comfortable taking out loans at low interest rates, and they will then use that money to boost the economy in the form of spending.

Countries around the world have similar national organizations that influence their business cycles. The Bank of Canada, the People's Bank of China, and the European Central Bank (representing countries in the financially linked European Union) are all examples of international institutions that have duties and powers like those of the U.S. Federal Reserve.

The National Bureau of Economic Research

The Fed has control over interest rates, and the United States government determines how much of the country's money is printed. Both of these acts affect contractions in the business cycle. However, the task of declaring a recession is typically left to a well-respected, privately owned, nonprofit organization called the National Bureau of Economic Research (NBER).

The NBER has built a solid reputation as a knowledgeable, influential force when it comes to shaping American economic

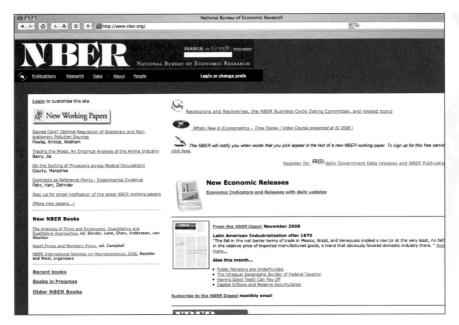

The National Bureau of Economic Research (http://www.nber.org) is a respected and influential resource when it comes to economic policy, analysis, and news.

policy and programs. In fact, the federal government looks to the bureau's Business Cycle Dating Committee to make the official determination as to whether or not a recession has taken place. The committee checks the economic situation on a monthly basis, not quarterly as other organizations do.

While paying close attention to the GDP, the committee also considers income, employment, and industrial production figures before announcing that the economy is in recession. Using these economic indicators, the committee identifies when the business cycle has peaked and exactly when it has hit a trough. The time between those two high and low points is what the NBER calls a recession.

Economic Indicators

In order to reach its conclusions regarding a recession, the NBER looks at sets of collected information known as economic indicators. They are called this because the data and statistics indicate, or point out, the direction of the economy.

You might think that when a slowdown is involved, indicators would also show a decline. But, this is not always the case. Economic indicators can be either procyclic or countercyclic. Procyclic indicators move in the same direction as the business cycle. During a recession, these statistics move downward along with the economy. Retail sales are an example of procyclic indicators. If sales figures are up, then the economy is expanding. When they fall, there is an economic contraction.

Countercyclic indicators, on the other hand, move in the opposite direction of the business cycle. This means that they increase or move upward during a slowdown. For instance, the number of people who are unemployed will rise as the business cycle contracts.

Shopping at the mall is more than a fun way to spend an afternoon. It can also give a boost to an ailing economy. Retail spending gives economists an indication of the economy's health.

Economic indicators are also time-sensitive, meaning they are closely connected to the past, present, or future. Lagging indicators show what has already happened in the business cycle. Coincident indicators give a clear picture of current

Key Economic Indicators

• **Gross domestic product (GDP)**—Perhaps the most reliable leading indicator, the GDP reveals overall buying and selling patterns on a monthly, quarterly, or yearly basis and moves in the same direction as the business cycle. Therefore, during an economic contraction, the GDP decreases.

Housing starts, which is what economists call new-home construction, are a leading economic indicator.

• **Unemployment figures**—A lagging indicator, unemployment numbers reflect entry into a recession but do not predict one.

• **Stock market**—Declining stock prices may signal an upcoming recession. Therefore, the performance of stock indices, like the Dow Jones Industrial Average or the Standard & Poor's 500, can be a leading indicator.

• **Consumer price index (CPI)**—A coincident indicator, the CPI tracks what customers are paying for goods and services.

• **Housing starts**—A leading indicator, this statistic measures the number of new homes that are built within a specific period, usually a month or a quarter.

• **Consumer confidence**—This leading indicator gauges how people feel about the economy and the security of their income, based on a survey of five thousand households. Low consumer confidence predicts a reduction in consumer spending.

economic activity. The most useful information comes from leading indicators, which indicate what is most likely to happen in the near future. By closely following leading indicators, economists and other advisers are better able to recognize a brewing recession and either stop it in its tracks or at least reduce the damage that results from a serious business-cycle contraction.

Whose Economic Indicators Can You Believe?

Not all collections of economic indicators are created equal. Several groups publish indicator lists, but the most trusted source for reliable data in America is the Joint Economic Committee (JEC) of the U.S. Congress. The committee is made up of twenty members—ten senators and ten members of the House of Representatives, from both major political parties.

Working with the Council of Economic Advisors—a group of economists who give input to the president on economic policy—the JEC analyzes indicators each month in seven categories. These are total output, income, and spending; employment, unemployment, and wages; production and business activity; prices; money, credit, and security markets; federal finance; and international statistics.

Another respected collection of economic statistics is the Index of Leading Economic Indicators (LEI). Compiled by the Conference Board, a nonprofit business research organization established in 1916, the LEI measures the business-cycle changes in nine countries, including the United States. The index factors in many things, including the average hours worked each week by manufacturing employees and the

The Joint Economic Committee often holds hearings to determine the state of the U.S. economy.

number of orders they fill, to the performance of the stock market and how confident consumers are in the health of their national economies.

Taken together, the indicators in the LEI reflect all the factors that influence the GDP. If the leading indicators show a decline for three months in a row, chances are good that the economy will enter a recession within the next twelve months.

CHAPTER FOUR
Real World Recessions

Recessions have been around for as long as there have been a money supply and the exchange of cash for goods and services. In ancient Rome, the government tried to increase its money supply by shaving silver from the edges of the denarius, which was the empire's coin money. The shavings were melted and made into new coins. Neither the original shaved coins nor the new ones contained as much silver as they should have, however, so the denarius literally lost a chunk of its value. The empire also tried mixing metals that weren't as precious as silver into coins, which made the denarius worth less as well.

The people of Rome started getting wise to what was happening. Merchants didn't trust the value of the denarius, so they started charging more for goods and services. Because there was so much devalued money circulating in the Roman economy, prices rose and the empire experienced inflation. The typical citizen's supply of money could not keep up with the increasing cost of living.

The Roman denarius frequently had an odd shape because of shaving. When coins were misshapen or felt lighter, citizens started to suspect that someone was cheating them.

Modern recessions haven't necessarily gone so far as to topple empires, but they have caused major disruptions to the normal business cycle, seriously harmed nations' fortunes, and affected millions of people.

Panic in the United States

The first major economic slowdown in America, known as the Panic of 1819, came after a period of expansion that followed the War of 1812. At that time, the country was filled with land speculators. These were men who borrowed money from banks and bought acreage so they could break the land into smaller lots and sell them quickly to make a profit. If the speculators didn't sell the land, there was a chance that the banks would not get back the money that they had given out as loans.

In order to buy the land, speculators took out loans from state and local banks. The Bank of the United States—which was the country's central bank at the time, an early version of the Federal Reserve—wanted to prevent state banks from making any more of these risky loans. As a result, it called in loans that it had made to the smaller banks. Without funds from the central bank, the state banks were forced to demand payment from the speculators on the credit and mortgage loans that had been given to them. Speculators who had not sold their landholdings could not make these payments. Many people lost their homes and were wiped out financially.

On top of the loan crisis, American exports, especially cotton to England, had declined rapidly. Other nations stopped buying U.S. goods, and Americans couldn't afford to buy much either. The slowdown in buying and selling created a recession. What followed were five years of massive unemployment, bank closings, and a drastic slowdown in the manufacturing and agriculture business sectors.

More Hard Times

Over the next century, the United States went through several additional recessions, including a downturn at the end of World War I in 1918. The economy soon rebounded after that, however. A strong business-cycle expansion took over during the first half of the appropriately nicknamed Roaring Twenties.

Even in the middle of this prosperity, though, there were troubling signs of economic problems in the United States. People and businesses borrowed heavily so they could spend lavishly. They also sank money into risky stock market investments. Consequently, money that should have been used to buy new items was instead spent on paying off debt or was lost entirely due to bad investments. By the mid-1920s, the country's GDP was shrinking, especially in the sectors of housing and durable goods (things like cars, appliances, furniture, and office equipment). American farmers also fell on hard times because there wasn't a strong demand for their products overseas. Without the income from exported food, many farmers couldn't afford to pay the mortgages on their land and homes.

All of these things contributed to the recession that eventually turned into the Great Depression, which began in 1929.

The economy was so good in the early 1920s that people were dancing in the streets—and on bridge railings. Joy turned to despair a few years later, however, when the Great Depression took hold for more than a decade.

For ten years, the world remained in this business-cycle trough. Military spending and increased industrial output in Europe and the United States at the start of World War II are largely credited with putting an end to the depression.

In the 1970s, the streets around America's gas stations began to look like parking lots as drivers lined up for hours to get scarce and expensive fuel.

Oil, Energy, and Inflation

After two minor slowdowns in the 1950s, recessions in America have occurred roughly every ten years. Each has

lasted anywhere from a few months to two years. The first in this series, a two-year recession that began in 1973, was the result of several factors. It was sparked by international political disagreements and a subsequent economic shock in the form of an oil shortage.

A group of predominantly Arab nations were part of an oil-producing alliance known as OPEC (Organization of Petroleum Exporting Countries). OPEC was, and remains, one of the main suppliers of the oil that is consumed in the United States. OPEC placed an embargo on the United States (an embargo is when trading with another nation is forbidden). The embargo completely shut off the sale of oil to the United States.

The lack of imported oil from the Middle East greatly

reduced the nation's supply of petroleum products, such as heating fuel and gasoline. People had to wait in long lines at gas stations. For a while, gas was rationed, meaning customers could buy only so many gallons during each trip to the pump. Because oil was now precious, its value rose, as did its price. Inflation took over. Money that should have been boosting the GDP through purchases in lots of different business sectors was instead being used to fill automobile and truck gas tanks and heat people's houses and businesses. When combined with years of heavy military spending on the war in Vietnam and higher than normal unemployment before the embargo, increasing prices soon drove the U.S. economy into a recession.

Recession in the 1990s

The late 1980s and early 1990s were an active, complex time for the U.S. economy. The country was dealing with a banking crisis, when hundreds of small savings and loan banks were failing, or going out of business, because of corruption and having made too many bad loans. America was also shaken by Black Monday on October 19, 1987, when the stock market experienced one of the largest single-day drops in history. Black Monday affected stock trading around the world.

Strangely enough, these events rattled the U.S. economy but did not immediately cause a recession. It would not be until almost three years later that the economy officially entered a recession. According to the Business Cycle Dating Committee, the 1990–1991 economic downturn was due to a decrease in manufacturing production and sales—one of the components of the GDP. Recall that the GDP is the total value of all

The stock market crash of 1987 was big news in the United States and around the world. Three years later, the country went into a recession.

goods and services produced in the country in a given period. The committee also noted dips in personal income and an increase in unemployment figures, but these indicators hadn't experienced clear troughs like the manufacturing numbers had.

A Burst Bubble

After the 1990–1991 recession, the U.S. economy experienced renewed expansion. It was being driven mainly by what was then a new business sector—Internet-based companies. Existing "brick-and-mortar" retail businesses found they could increase their sales by using advanced technology and the World Wide Web. They would sell their wares on the Web, in addition to or in place of traditional buying and selling in physical stores.

Buying and selling online became very popular. Hoping to take advantage of this situation and make a lot of money, businesspeople created hundreds of companies that specialized exclusively in online sales and computer technology. These were known as dot-coms because the new companies often had ".com" at the end of their names, which is Internet shorthand for "commerce."

Many investors bought stock in these new ventures. They were speculating that dot-coms would make large profits, causing their stock value to increase as well. Heavy investing created what is known as a stock bubble, where the price of stock in a certain business sector rises rapidly, sometimes regardless of the company's actual worth or the value of its products. The increased demand for the stock inflates the value of the stock and the perceived value and health of the company.

Corrupt business practices can be both a cause and a result of an economic recession. The arrest of company executives often occurs in advance of or during an economic crisis.

In their rush to make money, the owners of many dot-coms hadn't created very good business plans or even created any actual products to sell. They were simply selling the promise of a product that would eventually be offered and sold. Many of

Banks repossessing, or taking back, houses when people can not repay mortgage loans was a sure sign of economic problems in 2007 and beyond.

these companies built on flimsy foundations soon folded. Also, there were too many Internet-based companies on the market at one time, and there wasn't enough business to support them all. The supply of dot-coms far exceeded demand for their services,

so company values declined. By 2001, the technology stock bubble had burst. Stock prices fell, spending decreased, and many more Internet companies went out of business. The result was a stock market drop, a declining GDP, and an increase in unemployment figures as thousands of dot-com workers lost their jobs.

The recession that followed was also affected by the shock of the September 11 terrorist attacks on New York and Washington in 2001. Even after all this upheaval, though, the slowdown was relatively mild and, according to the NBER, lasted only eight months.

Housing and Credit Issues

In the early years of the twenty-first century, many Americans took advantage of low interest rates—which had been cut by the Fed to help kick-start the economy after the 2001 reces-sion—to take out loans, especially home mortgages. Knowing they could collect more money if they made more loans at lower interest rates, banks also lowered their mortgage interest rates and lending requirements. They even made subprime loans to people who were bad credit risks, although at higher interest rates. "Subprime" means that the borrower does not have a good credit rating and the loan is far riskier than an ordinary loan. Subprime loans used to be avoided or were care-fully insured in case the borrower could not pay back the loan. In the 2000s, however, subprime loans increased dramatically.

It became so easy to buy real estate that everyone wanted in on the action. Buyers also took advantage of the "easy money" banks were offering by using their homes as collateral to borrow even more money to make other big-ticket purchases (such as second homes, boats, or luxury cars). Collateral is valuable property that a borrower agrees to give to a lender if payments are not made on a loan. The value of houses went up as the demand increased, as did real estate prices. Unfortunately, personal income didn't rise to the same level. Soon, houses cost more than the average consumer could afford. By 2007, home sales dropped and borrowers defaulted on loans, meaning they failed to pay them back on time.

Complicating matters was the fact that groups of risky subprime mortgages were offered as a special kind of invest-ment opportunity, known as securities. Basically, outside investors gave banks the funds to cover these shaky loans, expecting in return to share the money from interest when the loans were repaid. When subprime borrowers defaulted, the investors lost money along with the banks. This caused a shake-up in stock markets worldwide, since international banks and

Ten Great Questions
to Ask a Financial Adviser

 1   What state is the economy in now, and how do you, personally, determine that?

 2   Given my income and expenses, how tight should my budget be?

 3   How much money should I be saving each month? What percentage of my income should be set aside?

 4   What form of savings is going to earn the most interest?

 5   When is the best time for me to make major purchases?

 6   What types of payment plans would you suggest for clearing up credit card debt?

 7   What business sectors offer the most job security during a recession?

 8   What investment strategy do you recommend during an economic slowdown?

 9   What advice have you given clients in the past that they say has helped them the most?

 10   How can I best plan for my financial future five, ten, twenty years down the road?

investors had purchased these securities. Even those investors who had stayed away from the securities became nervous because they were afraid their stocks and other investments would fail just like the subprime securities had. As a result, they made fewer new investments, even in relatively safe and healthy companies and projects.

Several indicators seemed to suggest that the economy was in a recession after these housing and credit difficulties. Stock market trading and the GDP dropped. Jobs were cut in the real estate, construction, and finance sectors, so unemployment rose. Yet, by the second half of 2008, the slowdown hadn't met either the two-consecutive-quarter or the NBER's "several months" definition of a recession. There was no arguing with one important indicator, though. Consumer confidence was very low. A majority of the American public believed that they were in the middle of a recession, and they were no longer spending their money. Finally, in November 2008, consumers' suspicions were confirmed. The United States—along with several other nations—was declared to have officially entered a recessionary period, one that was expected to be both deep and long-lasting.

CHAPTER FIVE

Dealing with the Effects of a Recession

Predicting a recession is tricky business. As part of the normal business cycle, recessions occur in the United States, on average, every five to ten years. The NBER states that in recent years, economic slowdowns have been cropping up less frequently than in decades past. According to Kenneth Rogoff of the International Monetary Fund, global recessions occur about as often, every eight to ten years. Beyond these facts, however, no one can be certain when the business cycle will contract, or how difficult a given contraction may be.

So how can governments and individuals prepare for a recession? By recognizing that these economic slowdowns are unavoidable, but suffering through them is not. Governments can introduce measures aimed at minimizing the effects of a recession before it starts while making sure that their own actions regarding the economy do not get out of control. Citizens need to pay close attention to the law of supply and demand in their own lives. They can try their best to live within their means—and encourage their government and elected officials to do the same. Both governments and ordinary citizens can best fight a recession by remaining calm, careful, and reasonable in their actions and reactions.

Returning money to taxpayers, known as a tax rebate, is a form of fiscal policy. The hope is that people will spend rebate checks that come from the Treasury.

Fiscal Policy

Economic policy is an attempt by a nation's government or central bank to influence the movements of the business

cycle. Policy is meant to be an intervention measure—getting involved in a positive way— rather than interference, which is negative and blocks progress.

There are two categories of policy that directly affect the economy: fiscal policy and monetary policy. Fiscal policy is the responsibility of law-makers and other government officials. In the United States, this includes the president and Congress. With fiscal policy, the government adds money to the economy in order to increase the demand for goods and services. The thinking is that people will spend more when there is more money available to them, thereby stimulating and expanding the economy.

Reducing taxes and increas-ing government spending are the two main fiscal policies that are used to insert money into

A Word About Subsidies

When a company is not able to make a profit, it is very discouraging for that business's owner and its employees. When whole groups of companies in a particular business sector don't turn a profit, it is bad news for the entire economy. When this happens, the government turns to a form of spending known as subsidies.

A subsidy is a government payment meant to encourage economic activity in a business or business sector that provides a necessary or unique product. When lack of profit threatens such an industry (like agriculture, steel, or automobile manufacturing), the government supports, or subsidizes, it with cash. This helps lower production costs and keeps the various companies within the industry in business.

the economy. Lowering the amount paid in taxes—through yearly income tax filings or sales tax on purchases—leaves more money available to spend in taxpayers' pockets. Tax rebates, in which the government sends checks to taxpayers as a way to get them to spend more, may also occur during a recession. This tactic was tried in 2001 and, most recently, in 2008.

Government spending, either directly on goods and services or through projects such as road and bridge construction, stimulates the economy in a different way. Government spending jump-starts production in various business sectors, creating more jobs and greater demand for goods and services. Money makes its way back into the economy through increased GDP and personal income.

The Monetary Policy Toolbox

Monetary policy is the responsibility of a country's central bank, which in the United States is the Federal Reserve. The goal of monetary policy is to stabilize employment levels and prices by influencing the availability of money and the affordability of borrowing and credit. To accomplish this, more money needs to be injected into the economy.

The Fed has three major tools that help set

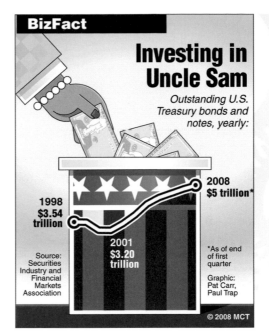

BizFact

Investing in Uncle Sam

Outstanding U.S. Treasury bonds and notes, yearly:

1998
$3.54 trillion

2001
$3.20 trillion

2008
$5 trillion*

*As of end of first quarter

Source: Securities Industry and Financial Markets Association

Graphic: Pat Carr, Paul Trap

© 2008 MCT

Buying U.S. Treasury bonds and T-bills is one of the safest investments a U.S. citizen can make. Another benefit is that this kind of investment is considered patriotic and helps the country pay for needed projects.

monetary policy in motion. Open market operations involve the buying and selling of government securities such as bonds and treasury bills (T-bills). Citizens buy these bonds and bills with the government's promise that, after holding on to them for a certain period of time, they will be worth more than the original price paid. It's like buying stock, only you're investing in the government instead of an individual company. Because they are backed by the U.S. government, bonds and T-bills are considered very safe investments. The money that the government raises by selling securities can be spent on all kinds of programs that would otherwise have to be funded by the raising of taxes.

During a recession, the government may buy back the securities it has sold, kind of like paying off an I.O.U. with interest. The money the government pays goes directly to the person who bought the securities. Most people will spend at least some of the money they earn from the sale of their securities back to the government, thus pumping much-needed money back into the economy.

Another monetary policy tool is a reduced interest rate on loans from the Fed to other banks. This is known as discount window lending because there is an actual teller's window at

High interest paid on credit card purchases adds greatly to personal debt. The government may lower interest rates during a recession in order to take some pressure off of consumers.

the Fed that other banks use when taking out discounted loans. It's similar to the commercial transactions window set aside for businesses at your local bank branch.

When the country is in a recession, the Fed wants to encourage borrowing from any source. Cutting interest rates on loans is one way to entice individuals, businesses, and even other banks to obtain credit and increase their ability to spend or invest. When the Fed cuts rates on loans to other banks, it is hoped that the banks will pass this savings on to its customers through similar cuts on credit cards and loans.

The Fed incorporates its third monetary policy tool by adding to or reducing reserves, which is money banks set aside from deposits as a security measure. This is a way to make sure banks have enough money on hand to cover depositor activity, such as making withdrawals and writing checks on their accounts.

Banks in the United States, including the Fed, are required to keep a percentage, or a fraction, of their total deposits in reserve. Money above and beyond the reserve requirement is available for lending, which stimulates the economy. To make sure this happens, the Fed may reduce the reserve rate requirement. So, if a bank has deposits equaling $1 million and the reserve rate is 20 percent, the reserve of cash that would have to be on hand would be $200,000. At a lower reserve rate of 10 percent, only $100,000 has to be held in reserve. The extra $100,000 deposited in the bank is now freed up for lending and the eventual spending or investing that will strengthen an economy.

Price Controls

Good economic policy can help shorten a recession and ease the problems associated with a slowdown. Bad economic policy,

In some countries of the world, price controls are set on basics, like milk, bread, butter, and toilet paper, to ensure that they remain affordable for average people.

on the other hand, can actually bring on a recession. One example of the latter type of policy involves price controls.

Price controls are a legal limit on how high prices in a certain business sector can rise. The limit is also called a cap.

Governments have used price controls frequently in the past to fight inflation. At first glance, it would seem that any policy aimed at keeping prices affordable would be a good thing. While price controls may help in the short term, they can disrupt the business cycle.

The reason has to do with the effect that fixing prices at a set amount has on production. Placing a cap on the price of a good or service keeps the cost low for consumers, which increases demand. As a result, businesses need more workers and materials to keep up with the increased demand. However, when price controls are in place, companies are not able to set higher prices that let them make a profit after increased expenses. Without that profit, they can't afford new employees or other higher production costs associated with increased production.

Eventually, these companies lose money. They either go out of business or switch to providing goods and services that don't have price controls and that allow them to make a healthy profit. Either way, the supply of the original price-controlled item decreases, even though demand from the public is still high. This negatively affects the natural flow of supply and demand, by imposing prices and quantities that are most likely not reflective of the true market forces.

Shoppers on a budget can make their money go further at stores that sell in bulk. Careful control of personal funds can help anyone weather a recession.

Protecting Yourself from a Recession

We've seen how governments handle a recession through economic policy. Now let's take a look at some personal policy measures you can take that will help you cope with an economic slowdown. While there's no way to become absolutely recession-proof, there are commonsense steps that you can take to protect your wealth and purchasing power.

Getting out of debt is the smartest thing you can do to fight the effects of a recession. Owing money is a huge drain on your finances. Pay as much as you can on your monthly credit card statement, not just the minimum. That way you avoid paying extra interest and other fees associated with carrying your debt from one month to the next.

Staying out of debt in the first place is also wise, so scale back on your spending. First, put yourself on a budget. This can be done on a monthly basis. Figure out how much money you bring home each month, after taxes. Then calculate how much you spend on necessities such as food, bills, and rent. Since some of these expenses will vary from month to month, you can add them and get an average. Once you write this information down, find areas of your budget that you can cut. Maybe you can eat at home more often, and you can rent movies instead of going to the cinema. In the areas where you must spend, such as food and gas, spend wisely. Be on the lookout for sales and the lowest prices, and take advantage of all discounts or rebates offered by manufacturers.

Other Important Considerations

What you do with the money you don't spend is just as important as budgeting the money you plan to spend. Open a savings account and put money into it as often as you can. Try to find one with a high interest rate that will allow your savings to grow steadily over time. Your savings can act as an emergency fund if you find yourself out of a job or otherwise struggling with cash during a recession. You can even take saving a step further by opening an IRA, which is a retirement account. Believe it or not, it's never too early to think about retirement and your financial future.

You can also make a few investments. A recession can be a good time to invest because the price of stocks and bonds is generally lower, which makes them easier to buy. This is sometimes referred to on Wall Street as bargain shopping. When the economy rebounds and starts to expand and stock prices begin to rise again, you are likely to earn money on your investment.

Speak with your parents, an economics professor, or a financial adviser to find out more about IRAs and investing. Safer investments usually involve long-established, financially sound companies that produce products or services that are likely to remain in demand for a very long time, during both economic good and bad times. These companies should also be putting a lot of their money and energy into research and development, signaling that they intend to stay at the leading edge of their industries.

Unemployment runs high during a recession, so if you don't already have a job, you may find it tough to get one. There are fewer jobs available when production is down. Consequently, not only will you have competition from others who are your own age, you may also be up against adults who have more experience but have been laid off because of the slowdown.

Get creative when trying to find work during a recession. Instead of holding out for your dream job, take a position that will let you progress to your ideal once the economy gets better. Think about part-time employment or starting your own business. Seek help from friends and family in finding leads in the field of your choice.

Creativity and patience aren't just helpful when trying to find work. Those traits, along with careful financial planning and industriousness, will help you get through even the longest lasting recessions. Stay flexible, work hard, save money in safe places, and spend carefully. If you do so, you will be well-positioned to roar back into financial life once the economy turns around again.

GLOSSARY

bubble In economics, a rapid rise in price and value.

business cycle The natural way the economy works, through a series of ups (expansions) and downs (contractions).

central bank A country's primary money authority.

circulation Currency moving freely through the economy; cash distributed to the public.

countercyclic Moving in the opposite direction of the business cycle.

depression A period of very low economic activity; a severe recession.

domino effect When one event sets off a chain of similar events, like lined-up dominoes that knock each other over.

economic indicators Data and statistics that indicate, or point out, the direction the economy is taking.

economic shocks Unpredictable events that affect the economy from the outside.

exports Goods and services a country sells to other nations.

globalization The development of connections between businesses and marketplaces around the world.

gross domestic product (GDP) The total value of all goods and services produced in the country in a given period of time, such as a month, a quarter (three months), or a year.

imports Goods and services that a country buys from other nations.

inflation A rise in the price level of goods and services.

interest The extra amount of cash paid as a sort of fee or service charge to the lender when money is borrowed. The interest charged is usually a certain percentage of the total loan amount.

lagging Falling behind.

menu costs The expenses associated with reprinting materials that list the prices of a business's offerings in order to reflect changes in the economy and rising costs.

procyclic Moving in the same direction as the business cycle.

recession When the economy experiences a slowdown, or contraction.

speculation Making risky investments in an attempt to make a quick profit.

stagnation When the economy shows no sign of moving down or up.

sticky prices Prices that can't change as quickly as the business cycle.

subprime loan A loan to a borrower with a weak credit history.

supply and demand A natural law that maps out how buyers and sellers act on their own and react to each other.

time-sensitive Describes information whose relevance is closely connected to either the past, present, or future.

FOR MORE INFORMATION

Bank of Canada
234 Wellington Street
Ottawa, ON K1A 0G9
Canada
Web site: http://www.bank-banque-canada.ca
As the country's central bank, the Bank of Canada is responsible
for the national financial system, including monetary
policy, bank notes, and fund management.

Board of Governors of the Federal Reserve System
20th Street and Constitution Avenue NW
Washington, DC 20551
Web site: http://www.federalreserve.gov
The Federal Reserve System is the central bank of the United
States. The Federal Reserve's duties include conducting the
nation's monetary policy, supervising and regulating banking
institutions, maintaining the stability of the financial system,
and providing financial services to depository institutions,
the U.S. government, and foreign official institutions.

Bureau of Economic Analysis
1441 L Street NW
Washington, DC 20230
(202) 606-9900

Web site: http://www.bea.gov/bea/role.htm

An agency of the U.S. Department of Commerce, the Bureau of Economic Analysis provides timely, relevant, and accurate economic statistics and data.

Department of the Treasury
1500 Pennsylvania Avenue NW
Washington, DC 20220
(202) 622-2000
Web site: http://www.ustreas.gov

The Treasury Department is the executive agency responsible for promoting economic prosperity and ensuring the financial security of the United States. The department is responsible for a wide range of activities, such as advising the president on economic and financial issues, encouraging sustainable economic growth, and fostering improved governance in financial institutions. The Department of the Treasury operates and maintains systems that are critical to the nation's financial infrastructure, such as the production of coin and currency, the disbursement of payments to the American public, revenue collection, and the borrowing of funds necessary to run the federal government.

National Bureau of Economic Research
1050 Massachusetts Avenue
Cambridge, MA 02138-5398
(617) 868-3900
Web site: http://www.nber.org

The NBER is a private, nonprofit, nonpartisan research organization dedicated to promoting a greater understanding of how the American economy works.

National Council on Economic Education
1140 Avenue of the Americas
New York, NY 10036
(212) 730-7007 or (800) 338-1192
Web site: http://www.ncee.net
Through programs and publications, the NCEE helps students
    think and choose responsibly as consumers, savers, investors,
    citizens, members of the workforce, and effective participants
    in a global economy.

The Peter G. Peterson Institute for International Economics
1750 Massachusetts Avenue NW
Washington, DC 20036-1903
(202) 328-9000
Web site: http://www.iie.com
A private, nonprofit research organization, the Peterson Institute
    is devoted to the study of international economic policy.

Web Sites

Due to the changing nature of Internet links, Rosen Publishing
has developed an online list of Web sites related to the subject
of this book. This site is updated regularly. Please use this link
to access the list:

http://www.rosenlinks.com/rwe/rece

FOR FURTHER READING

Adil, Janeen R. *Supply and Demand* (First Facts). Mankato, MN: Capstone Press, 2006.

Allman, Barbara. *Banking* (How Economics Works). Minneapolis, MN: Lerner Publications, 2005.

Apel, Melanie Ann. *The Federal Reserve Act: Making the American Banking System Stronger*. New York, NY: Rosen Publishing Group, 2006.

Boyd, Bentley. *Comix Economix*. Williamsburg, VA: Chester Comix, 2003.

Craats, Rennay. *Economy* (USA Past, Present, Future). New York, NY: Weigl Publishers, 2008.

Economist Newspaper, Ltd. *Guide to Economic Indicators: Making Sense of Economics*. New York, NY: Bloomberg Press, 2007.

Gilman, Laura Anne. *Economics* (How Economics Works). Minneapolis, MN: Lerner Publications, 2006.

Harman, Hollis Page. *Money Sense for Kids*. Hauppauge, NY: Barron's Educational Series, 2005.

McGraw-Hill. *Economics: Today and Tomorrow*. Student Edition. New York, NY: Glencoe/McGraw-Hill, 2007.

O'Sullivan, Arthur, and Steven M. Sheffrin. *Economics: Principles in Action*. Upper Saddle River, NJ: Pearson Prentice Hall, 2006.

BIBLIOGRAPHY

Business Cycle Dating Committee. "NBER Business Cycle Dating Committee Determines That Recession Ended in March 1991." National Bureau of Economic Research, December 1992. Retrieved August 2008 (http://www.nber.org/March91.html).

Clayton, Gary E. *Economics: Principles and Practices.* Westerville, OH: Glencoe/McGraw-Hill, 2004.

Gandel, Stephen. "Survival Strategies: Recession-Proof Your Life." CNNMoney.com, February 2008. Retrieved August 2008 (http://money.cnn.com/2008/02/08/pf/recession_proof.moneymag).

Gereffi, Gary. "The Global Economy: Organization, Governance, and Development." *Handbook of Economic Sociology.* Princeton, NJ: Princeton University Press, 2004.

Gongloff, Mark. "Did Recession Begin in 2000?" CNNMoney.com, January 2004. Retrieved August 2008 (http://money.cnn.com/2004/01/22/news/economy/nber/index.htm).

Gross, Daniel. "Why It's Worse Than You Think." *Newsweek,* June 16, 2008, pp. 20–30.

Hall, Robert, et al. "The NBER's Recession Dating Procedure." The National Bureau of Economic Research, January 7, 2008. Retrieved August 2008 (http://www.nber.org/cycles/jan08bcdc_memo.html).

Maybury, Richard J. *Whatever Happened to Penny Candy?*
    Placerville, CA: Bluestocking Press, 2004.

Moffatt, Mike. "A Beginner's Guide to Economic Indicators."
    About.com. Retrieved June 2008 (http://economics.
    about.com/cs/businesscycles/a/economic_ind.htm?p=1).

Reynolds, Alan. "Economic Hysteria." *New York Post*, April 11,
    2008. Retrieved August 2008 (http://www.nypost.com/
    seven/04112008/postopinion/opedcolumnists/economic_
    hysteria_106074.htm).

Rogoff, Kenneth. "The Recession That Almost Was."
    International Monetary Fund. *Financial Times*, April 5,
    2002. Retrieved August 2008 (http://www.imf.org/
    external/np/vc/2002/040502.htm).

Schiffman, Betsy. "'Pervasive' Recession Won't Repeat Dot-Com
    Bust, Experts Say." *Wired*, March 2008. Retrieved
    August 2008 (http://www.wired.com/techbiz/startups/
    news/2008/03/dotcom_repeat).

INDEX

About the Author

Jeanne Nagle is familiar with life during an economic slowdown. She had lined up to buy gas in the 1970s, struggled to find full-time work in the early 1990s, seen her investments dwindle in 2001, and been unable to afford property due to the recent housing bubble. Her training as a journalist allows her to put these experiences in context and speak with authority on the nature of recessions.

Photo Credits

Cover (top) © www.istockphoto.com/Andrey Prokhorov; cover (middle) © www.istockphoto.com/Lilli Day; cover (bottom) © Stan Honda/AFP/Getty Images; p. 1 © Mario Tama/Getty Photos; pp. 6–7 © www.istockphoto.com/Kris Hanke; p. 9 © Franck Fife/AFP/Getty Images; pp. 10–11 © David McNew/Getty Images; pp. 14–15 © Carl De Souza/AFP/Getty Images; pp. 16–17, 28 © Bettmann/Corbis; p. 21 Rick Gershon/Getty Images; p. 25 © Kyle Niemi/U.S. Coast Guard via Getty Images; pp. 26–27, 40, 46–47 © AP Photos; p. 29 © www.istockphoto.com/Corstiaan van Elzelingen; pp. 32–33 © www.istockphoto.com/Bryan Faust; pp. 36–37 © www.istockphoto.com/Dimitrly Shironosov; pp. 38, 52–53 © Justin Sullivan/Getty Images; p. 42 © The Trustees of the British Museum/Art Resource, N.Y.; p. 45 Library of Congress Prints and Photographs Division; p. 49 © James Marshall/Corbis; p. 51 © Stuart Ramson/Getty Images; pp. 58–59 © Jeff Fusco/Getty Images; p. 61 © Newscom; p. 62 © www.istockphoto.com/Marcus Clackson; pp. 64–65 © Peter Turnley/Corbis; pp. 66–67 © GabrielBuoys/AFP/Getty Images.

Designer: Sam Zavieh; Photo Researcher: Marty Levick